# HOW TO PRAY WHEN YOU DON'T HAVE TIME

DEBRA D. JONES

*How to Pray When You Don't Have Time*

Copyright © 2016 by Debra D Jones

Editing by Val Pugh-Love

All rights reserved. This book or any portion thereof may not be reproduced or used in any manner whatsoever without the express written permission of the publisher except for the use of brief quotations in a book review.

All Scripture references are from the NIV unless otherwise noted and are from the public domain.

Printed in the United States of America

First Printing, 2016

ISBN: 978-0-9975563-0-8

*I dedicate this book to the memories of my mother, Mildred H. Jones-Lloyd who taught us by example that we always have time for prayer and the memory of my godmother, Missionary LaRuth Betty Johnson who never got tired of praying.*

# ACKNOWLEDGMENTS

This book could not have been completed without the love, support, and inspiration of my Lord and Savior Jesus Christ.

Thanks to my husband and son, Bill and Mike Jones. God blessed me with both of you, and I am forever grateful for your encouragement and support. Thank you for loving me and working with me during my evolution from who I was to being a Daughter of the King of Kings! I love you both forever and ever and ever and ever...

I thank Dr. Jinneh Dyson for her support, direction, resources, and coaching throughout the writing process and her ability to help me to ThinkUP! and write the core of this book in 30 days!

To my sister in the Gospel and oldest sibling, Minister Vivian J. Gipson who activated me as an intercessor when I didn't know that I was an intercessor, thank you for asking me to pray for you when we always depended on you to pray for us.

To my big sister Patricia (PJ) Jones, an awesomely gifted writer and encourager, thank you for believing in my ability to write, copyrighting my manuscript and pushing me to publish! I look forward to the world enjoying your published writings as well.

To my other siblings, Claude Jr., Ronald, Robert, Richard, and Brenda, thank you for your love and support and for always looking out for your baby sister.

To my Pastors and Spiritual parents, Drs. John and Evelyn Ogletree of First Metropolitan Church in Houston, Texas, thank you for your training, support, and covering.

To Pastor J.P. and Missionary Novella Augustine (Dad and Mother) of True Vine Church of God in Christ in Houston, Texas, thank you for showing me the way to salvation and holiness.

To every writing coach at whose feet I learned how to take the gifts God has given me and increase them through my writing, thank you.

To all my friends, family, colleagues, social media friends, and especially to my Periscope 'Can You Pray 5 Minutes?' family, Thank You!

# CONTENTS

| | |
|---|---|
| Introduction | 1 |
| | |
| Faith – I Failed, But I'm Getting Up | 3 |
| Faith – Live | 7 |
| Faith – On Your Mark | 11 |
| Faith – What are You Waiting For? | 15 |
| Faith – Who Killed Hope? | 19 |
| Faith – Work | 23 |
| | |
| Family – Family Feuds | 27 |
| Family – Forgive Again | 31 |
| Family – The Happy Life | 35 |
| Family – The Measure of Success | 39 |
| Family – The Secret Place | 43 |
| Family – Who is My Family? | 47 |
| | |
| Fear – Yes You Can | 51 |
| Fear – The Test | 55 |
| Fear – Sending a Shout Out to Fear | 59 |
| Fear – More Than I Asked For | 63 |
| Fear – Just Do It | 67 |
| Fear – Dig it Up | 71 |
| | |
| Finances – Generosity | 75 |
| Finances – God 1st | 79 |
| Finances – Mikey Rich | 83 |
| Finances – Old Math | 87 |
| Finances – Pinching Pennies | 91 |
| Finances – Work | 95 |
| | |
| Life – Earn, Learn or Free | 99 |
| Life – Open Mouth, Insert Foot | 103 |
| Life – iCan | 107 |
| Life – iWill | 111 |
| Life – iMust | 115 |
| Life – The Help | 119 |
| Day 31 – The Prayer | 133 |

# FOREWORD

## By Dr. Jinneh Dyson

*How To Pray When You Don't Have Time* is the life-changing solution to many of our biggest challenges. This book is a must-have tool for every "busy" person who yearns for a more powerful and impactful prayer life, but whom feels that they lack the time. Tailored with the perfect words and practical scenarios that mirror our daily lives, this book is destined to inspire us to revamp and shift how we live each and every day. Debra has captured and translated her own REAL life experiences to help strengthen our innermost spiritual beings.

Her passion is to teach and transform how we think and perceive prayer. She is a believer of living on purpose and uses her vast knowledge and experiences to help others excel in their own divine purposes.

Through vulnerability and transparency this book encourages us all to dig deeper and to reach back into our own arsenals of self-development and our very own prayer closets. Time is our greatest currency, and prayer is our most powerful weapon. Debra believes that prayer even as little as five minutes a day can change your mere existence. So are you still believing you don't have time? If so, then this book is the perfect auxiliary for your life.

# INTRODUCTION

*How to Pray When You Don't Have Time* is a daily devotional that addresses areas of Faith, Family, Fear, Finances as well as others in an easy-read fashion. If your days are so busy that it resembles one extremely long run-on sentence because you are a leader, parent, sibling, employee, employer, entrepreneur, friend, thought leader, student, encourager, ministry worker, among other titles, then this book is for you. Each topic over a 30-day span has a scenario, scripture reference, and a short prayer. Day 31 is a prayer written for you that you can add to and personalize. At the completion of this devotional, I believe you will find that your relationship with spending time with the Father is enhanced, your day is blessed, and issues that most Christians face daily can be addressed within the Word of God.

Begin your journey of spending the most important time of your day with your Heavenly Father set aside for Him within the pages of this devotional.

Debra D Jones

# Day 1

**Proverbs 24:16**

# DAY 1
# FAITH: I FAILED, BUT I'M GETTING UP

Humans make mistakes. In fact, some of us make the same mistakes more than once. If we focus on failing, we may even beat ourselves up and decide that whatever it is, it is not something that we can do well. Furthermore, we may even define ourselves by the event. I'm sure you've said, "I cannot complete this exercise, I cannot succeed in this area, or I'm no good at this." Trust me, I've been there. However, what I can tell you is that although I've not always come out initially with a desired outcome in many different areas of my life, I have not stayed at that juncture. Yes, I failed, but I am not a failure.

I made a career change that requires me to speak in front of large groups. Public speaking as a career for me came as a great surprise to many, including myself. One of the biggest mistakes I made during the initial presentation to determine if I would be able to continue on my new career path was that I spent too much time thinking about what I was doing and saying instead of making the presentation as myself, in my own voice, in my own personality. I knew immediately that my presentation sucked, but I didn't know how to fix it. Meanwhile, I waited to hear from my boss about how my presentation was received.

Well, he eventually gave me the news, and I had indeed failed. He also told me he knew I was capable of doing a much better job. Therefore, he went to bat for me so I would be given another chance! Thank God for another chance and FAVOR!!! (That's an entirely different message.)

The next time I made my presentation, I had nothing to lose. I did it fearlessly. I presented it without trying to hit all the points others would hit, without saying the words others would say, without worrying about whether I was good enough… I did it with a prayer in my heart asking God for His help, and I used my voice, my personality, and my words. It was probably one of the best presentations I've ever made. To God be the glory. Failing doesn't have to be the last stop for you. It can simply serve as a training field for your success!

### Scripture Reference: Proverbs 24:16

"For though the righteous fall seven times, they rise again, but the wicked stumble when calamity strikes."

### Prayer:

*Heavenly Father, it is not my desire to disappoint you. Help me to walk worthy of being your child. When I fail in any area, give me the ability to recover quickly. In Jesus' name. Amen.*

## Reflections

# Day 2

**Ezekiel 37:4-5**

# DAY 2
# FAITH—LIVE

My family loves to host and entertain. We love serving others, and I get a kick out of making sure we have a nice atmosphere in our home when we do so. Sometimes that atmosphere includes freshly cut flowers. On one occasion, I planned to buy freshly cut flowers, but I purchased two orchids instead. They were beautiful. One of them had white blooms, and the other one had pink. I placed them on a table in our house and took them to work the following Monday so I could enjoy them there.

When I arrived at work, I placed the orchids in the window in my office where they remained until their blooms fell off. The once beautiful plants now looked like two sticks to me. At this point, I put both plants in the trash. My manager stopped by my office and saw them in the trash and asked why they were there. I told him, "They're dead." He informed me that they were not dead, but that it was a season of rest for the blooms. He took them back to his office and fed, watered, and nurtured them for an entire year! I was amazed by how they looked when I visited his office.

One day, my manager stopped by to return one of the plants to me. The stick that I placed in the trash that originally had two blooms now had at least six beautiful blooms. Those blooms were at least twice as large and much more beautiful than they were when I purchased the plants. I learned a lot from those plants. There are times when people and situations look like they're dead, but they are actually in a state of rest. Their season for blooming may have passed, and they may need additional feeding, watering, and nurturing. However, if there is breath in their bodies, they can live again. Today I say to you: LIVE!

### Scripture Reference: Ezekiel 37:4-5

"⁴Then he said to me, "Prophesy to these bones and say to them, 'Dry bones, hear the word of the Lord! ⁵ This is what the Sovereign Lord says to these bones: I will make breath enter you, and you will come to life."

### Prayer:

*Heavenly Father, when I look through natural eyes, it is sometimes difficult for me to see what you see. Open my eyes to see clearly and let me not count anything as dead that still has life. Teach me your ways. In Jesus' name. Amen.*

## *Reflections*

# Day 3

**Psalm 27:14**

# DAY 3
# FAITH—ON YOUR MARK

On your mark.
Get set.
Not yet.

Ah ah ah, don't take off before you've heard, "Go!"

When we have an idea or notion, we often think about moving in faith and just doing it. Faith is absolutely the substance of things hoped for and the evidence of things not seen, (Hebrews 11:1) but there are times that God has clearly indicated to you that it's not time to go. How can you be sure? Ask God. If He doesn't give you the indication of a clear start, don't go. If you're starting a business, He may delay you a bit until the market changes so you'll be able to purchase materials for the business at a greatly discounted rate. If you're planning to go back to school, He may be setting you up for a scholarship that will take care of what you'd have to sacrifice greatly to pay for. If you're planning to marry someone that you believe is the one, He may be allowing you to delay the wedding so you will know that the person is a counterfeit or that you're still too concerned about yourself to become one with anyone else.

There are times when we just need to wait for His signal to go. In sports, if you move before the signal is given, there may be a warning, penalty or immediate disqualification. I believe we can see the same with God. Sometimes He's merciful and gives us a warning. Other times, we pay for moving too quickly. Moreover, there are still times when you're disqualified for the blessing that was coming because you moved too quickly. God doesn't want you to become so cautious that you are afraid of operating in faith, and you end up overthinking everything and miss the timing. Be sure that you ask God for the time and direction He wants you to move in. It'll prevent you from suffering a false start.

### Scripture Reference: Psalm 27:14 KJV

"Wait on the Lord: be of good courage, and he shall strengthen thine heart: wait, I say, on the Lord."

### Prayer:

*Father, my desire is to please you. Sometimes my timing is off. As I spend more time with you, I am learning to hear you more clearly. Open my ears so I can hear what Holy Spirit is saying. In Jesus' name. Amen.*

## *Reflections*

# Day 4

**Deuteronomy 1:6-8**

# DAY 4
# FAITH—WHAT ARE YOU WAITING FOR?

I'm waiting for the next move... I've heard this many times and can even confess that I've said it as well when the question has come up about what I'm going to do concerning a dream, a new career, a promotion, a direction in ministry, etc. There are absolutely times when we need to wait because things are not in order for what we need to accomplish. The timing may be wrong, it could be the wrong season, the finances are not in place, or our character may be being built. There could be many reasons why we haven't moved. However, more often than not the next move is waiting for you. It could be that fear, laziness, or procrastination is getting in the way and stifling your progression. Ask God if it's okay for you to move, and examine yourself to see if this is the problem.

I waited more than two decades before I made a career change. I wanted to do it before that, but I wasn't sure if the time was right, if I knew enough, if I could make it, if my husband would agree, or if we would have enough money to live comfortably if things didn't work out. Then, one day I decided to just jump! I've made a few mistakes along the way, things have not always been perfect, but I can tell you this...it was well worth it! I realize now that I was ready long before I made that leap. What I didn't know then is that I would learn more during the journey. You may be someone who is waiting until you believe you are an expert in your field before you move to the next level. The truth is once you become an expert, you may in fact be overqualified for the next assignment but not have any notable progressive experience. Ask God, take a chance, and seek the next level. It likely will present unexpected challenges, but you can do it. Move to the next level and watch yourself succeed!

**Scripture Reference: Deuteronomy 1:6-8**

"⁶ The Lord our God said to us at Horeb, "You have stayed long enough at this mountain. ⁷ Break camp and advance into the hill country of the Amorites; go to all the neighboring peoples in the Arabah, in the mountains, in the western foothills, in the Negev and along the coast, to the land of the Canaanites and to Lebanon, as far as the great river, the Euphrates. ⁸ See, I have given you this land. Go in and take possession of the land the Lord swore he would give to your fathers—to Abraham, Isaac and Jacob—and to their descendants after them."

**Prayer:**

*Father, I've made so many excuses about why I haven't taken care of your business. I am at the point where I can admit that. I look to you for a solution to prevent me from going back to those old ways of procrastinating. Please keep me focused on You, and help me to finish assignments in the time frame you set. In Jesus' name. Amen.*

## *Reflections*

# Day 5

**Romans 4:18**

# DAY 5

# FAITH—WHO KILLED HOPE?

Jesse Jackson delivered a powerful speech at the 1988 Democratic National Convention titled "Keep Hope Alive." That title has resonated with me all these years later because I realize that hope can be a great motivator that keeps us going. When we walk in faith, we are in a state of belief based on evidence of things not seen. What happens when we're having difficulty in faith (help my unbelief), cannot see, and have nothing else? Hope keeps us going even when our faith is struggling. Hope will assure against everything that things will work out for our good.

I have a beautiful sister friend who said, concerning medical treatment she receives, "Deb, there were times that I was ready to give up. I didn't feel like myself anymore, but I can honestly say I now have hope." Let me tell you I felt like doing a dance, because although I was praying and believing God for her healing, I believed her hope was essential to her participation in what God wanted to do for her. Hope says although I can't see it and can't fathom how it will work out, my faith has weakened to the point that it is above my imagination level. I know it can work out and I'm anticipating it!

Doubt is the antonym of hope and loves to try to overwhelm us with negative imaginations, words, and notions.  Let's put a hit out on doubt today and assassinate it so that hope lives freely!   For anyone that is reading this today, remember that hope is alive and well because of Jesus' finished work on the cross.  Live today to its fullest as we celebrate the life of hope!

### Scripture Reference: Romans 4:18

"Against all hope, Abraham in hope believed and so became the father of many nations, just as it had been said to him, "So shall your offspring be."

### Prayer:

*Father, if hope is all I have, I know you are all I need.  I will look to you for everything else. In Jesus' name. Amen.*

## *Reflections*

# Day 6

**James 2:17**

# DAY 6
# FAITH—WORK

To the human mind that is familiar with operating to achieve results based on facts, faith may serve as one of the most difficult things to do. With faith being the substance of things hoped for and evidence that has not been seen, you may wonder: "How can it be verified that faith is actually working?" Well, faith requires extreme reliance and trust in God and His ability to perform and bring to pass the things that are appropriate for the situation or circumstance.

Years ago I had a dream that I was in a room with an open window. I had made it to this room because I was being pursued (by who or what, I cannot be sure, but I do not believe it was a friendly force). After a quick glance around the room, I decided the only exit was the window. The area outside the window was so foggy that I could not see past my own hand. I decided to go outside the window, and I connected with a bar, very similar to what a monkey bar on a playground would look like. I started to move by swinging from bar to bar with my hands…left hand connected, then right hand, left hand connected, then right hand…

I was making steady progress when I realized that the bars that I was connecting with would only appear when I reached out and grabbed them! They were not there before. I also realized that I was very high up; I could not even see the ground below me. I started to question God: "Lord, how am I able to move and connect with these bars?" Then, I heard Him say, "That's the way faith works. It manifests when you act on it." The Lord also reassured me that if I fell from that height, He was able to catch me! Faith has requirements that I can fulfill on my end by putting in work and knowing that God is able to support me from any height.

### Scripture Reference: James 2:17

"In the same way, faith by itself, if it is not accompanied by action, is dead."

### Prayer:

*Father, I will continue to have faith in you. As I add works to my faith, I expect results because of You. In Jesus' name. Amen.*

## *Reflections*

# Day 7

John 13:34

# DAY 7
# FAMILY—FAMILY FEUDS

I grew up in a family with a total of eight children - four boys and four girls. We didn't have a lot of material possessions, but there was never a dull moment. With all those children under the same roof, there was a lot of fun and laughter, great memories, and general warmth in our home. There were also times when one or more of the siblings had conflict with each other. My mother would intervene and tell us to make up. It wasn't optional; we had to make up. We would reluctantly do so and move on about our business. It was hard to keep conflict going in a small space with so many people. Over time, we all learned the art of conflict resolution without my mother's intervention.

One of the things I realize when I look back is that we resolved conflicts because we were told to, but there was an added reason: We love each other, and anyone that knows our family, knows about our genuine love for one another.

As Christians, we are commanded to love one another. Commands are required actions. They are not optional. This is one of the ways that we can be identified as members of the body of Christ. Check your love game with your family today. If it's not strong, seek God on how you're able to strengthen it with His help.

**Scripture Reference: John 13:34**

"A new command I give you: Love one another. As I have loved you, so you must love one another."

**Prayer:**

*Heavenly Father, thank you for demonstrating true love with your son, Jesus. I will love even when it is difficult. In Jesus' name. Amen.*

## *Reflections*

# Day 8

**Luke 17:3-4**

# DAY 8
# FAMILY—FORGIVE AGAIN

In the traditional sense, family would be those connected to you by common biological ancestry. Family may also be those that are members of the body of Christ who are related to you because they accepted Christ as Savior. You now share the same DNA with them because of the Blood of Christ. Have you ever felt like your family has done you wrong? Perhaps they lied on, cheated on, misused, or abused you. What do you do when the very ones that are closely connected to you cause you to distrust them? The Word of God says to rebuke them, and if they repent, forgive them.

To forgive means you stop feeling angry or resentful towards them. I can hear some of you saying, "I don't trust them because of what they've done!" Trust is not the same as forgiveness. You may be correct in being careful with placing confidence in their abilities based on their character and the discernment given by God. However, what happens if they have the opportunity and sin against you again? Use the same formula: Rebuke them, and if they repent, forgive them. The act of forgiving them is prescribed by God and will be a blessing to you as you will not bear the burden of unforgiveness. Try forgiving family today.

### Scripture Reference: Luke 17:3-4

"³So watch yourselves. If your brother or sister sins against you, rebuke them; and if they repent, forgive them. ⁴Even if they sin against you seven times in a day and seven times come back to you saying 'I repent,' you must forgive them."

### Prayer:

*Father, you have forgiven me more times than I can count. Help me perfect my forgiveness. In Jesus' name. Amen.*

## *Reflections*

# Day 9

**Proverbs 21:9; 25:24**

# DAY 9
# FAMILY—THE HAPPY LIFE

Happy wife, happy life. I've heard this statement many times before. I can admit that I may have even made the statement at some point in my marriage. Generally, when this statement is made it alludes to the idea that if a husband can make sure his wife is happy, she will not make his life unhappy. When I looked at what God wants to happen in marriage, it became my goal to try to not be the source of my husband's unhappiness. I've noticed in general that men are not interested in a lot of arguments and confrontations. They tend to like peaceful environments. If a man's home is to be his castle, peace should be one of the main things in his home.

If you are a current wife, wife-in-training or wife-in-waiting, your husband's peace and happiness is important. It would not be good for a husband to prefer to spend time in a small place (corner) in an environment open to the elements (roof) than to be in the same house with you because you like to be quarrelsome (also defined as petty) or disagree about any and every thing. If you are able to see yourself as I did in any of the above, now that you know better, let's work on being better.

### Scripture Reference: Proverbs 21:9, Proverbs 25:24

"Better to live on a corner of the roof than share a house with a quarrelsome wife."

### Prayer:

*Father, I want to be a wife whose husband is happy and not grieved because of me being petty. Help me recognize the parts of me that are not like you. When I feel like being disagreeable, please step in so my husband can see you through me. In Jesus' name. Amen.*

## *Reflections*

# Day 10

**Psalm 63: 2-8**

# DAY 10

# FAMILY—THE MEASURE OF SUCCESS

I love spending time with family laughing, enjoying and creating memories. I treasure some of the smallest things that happen when we are together, and I am always looking for ways to spend time doing things that will bring joy to my loved ones. I promised one of my young nieces that I would give her a tea party. Time kept getting in the way. There was always something else that demanded my attention and I couldn't coordinate my time off to make it happen. One day my niece and a few other family members were at my house, and I said "Why don't we have a tea party now?" My young niece was excited and agreed. I pulled out my special teacups and spoons along with cubes of sugar. I quickly made tea and poured it from one of the teapots that I collect.

We sat and continued to enjoy each other's company while sipping our tea at the hastily arranged tea party. When we were finished, I put the teacups and spoons away as well as the few items that were put together for the impromptu tea party. Then, my young niece said "Auntie, the tea party was a success!" I could hardly believe my ears and contain my great joy. What I wanted to arrange for my niece was a lavish tea party with specially folded napkins, little sandwiches, girls in their spring dresses and hats, as well as gloves and fruit cut in fancy shapes and served on fancier plates. That was my idea of what a successful tea party would look like.

What I learned that day from my niece is that all she wanted was to spend time with me having tea. Since we were able to accomplish that, she declared the tea party a success. I believe there are times that we measure success by what we think it should look like - including the time that we spend with God. He wants to spend time with us because He loves us. We are His family, and when we spend that time in fellowship with Him whether it's for hours on end or a few precious moments throughout the day, the quality of our time together is declared successful.

## Scripture Reference: Psalm 63:2-8

"[2] I have seen you in the sanctuary and beheld your power and your glory. [3] Because your love is better than life, my lips will glorify you. [4] I will praise you as long as I live, and in your name I will lift up my hands. [5] I will be fully satisfied as with the richest of foods; with singing lips my mouth will praise you. [6] On my bed I remember you; I think of you through the watches of the night. [7] Because you are my help, I sing in the shadow of your wings. [8] I cling to you; your right hand upholds me."

## Prayer:

*Father, our time together is special to me. I love when you speak to me and hold me close. Help me to not make spending time with you difficult by making it a difficult production. I love you. In Jesus' name. Amen.*

## *Reflections*

# Day 11

**Psalm 91:1-2**

# DAY 11
# FAMILY—THE SECRET PLACE

My husband is a great chef, and our family loves to entertain guests in our home. Generally, on a holiday or birthday celebration, there is plenty of food prepared and great conversations shared. Before we begin to eat, we will stand with all in attendance and the elder that is present or an appointee will pray a blessing. Then, the line forms to make plates, get something to drink, and find a seat in the kitchen, living area, patio or den area to sit, eat, and fellowship. Our repeat guests know that they do not need to call ahead to add a plus one, there is always enough for whoever stops by. We have hosted family and friends alike, and many guests have shared that they feel welcome. Some may stay long into the day. One friend told us that people don't want to leave because they feel so welcome. We are grateful that our hospitality is evident and people feel at ease.

As our guests mingle and enjoy one another's company, they are welcome throughout our home, but there is one room that always has a closed door. It is the door to our master bedroom. Our master bedroom represents a private place reserved for my husband and me. In fact, not many of our guests can say that they've ever been inside our master bedroom. We reserve our master bedroom for ourselves as a place of rest, refuge, and intimacy. Conversations there have an unspoken 'this is between us' disclaimer. God has a place that we can retreat to as well. That is a place of intimacy with the Master. His door is open to those that wish to go deeper in their relationship with Him where we can find rest, refuge, and trust.

### Scripture Reference: Psalm 91:1-2

"[1] Whoever dwells in the shelter of the Most High will rest in the shadow of the Almighty. [2] I will say of the LORD, "He is my refuge and my fortress, my God, in whom I trust."

### Prayer:

*Father, thank you for a special place to share with the one that I am closest to. Thank you for creating a sanctuary for us. In Jesus' name. Amen.*

## *Reflections*

# Day 12

**Mark 3:35**

# DAY 12
# FAMILY—WHO IS MY FAMILY?

Tracing family genealogy and history has become very popular in modern times. DNA home test kits are available at local pharmacies and promise to supply the subject being tested with scientific genetic information contained in chromosomes that can help pinpoint their ancestry. Perhaps the information can even help connect the subject being tested with relatives that they never knew existed. I find the information very interesting and intriguing to hear of stories of people that did not realize some of their relatives were from ethnic groups that they never imagined. I also love to hear of the stories of family members that meet for the very first time and realize that they have crossed paths their entire lives. Although their cultural upbringings may have been as different as night and day, many of these newly found family members often share similar mannerisms and aptitudes that cannot always be explained scientifically.

Have you met someone whose upbringing and background was very different from yours, but you felt an immediate kinship with the person? This has been my story on a number of occasions. Within a few minutes of conversation, it's as if the results have been received from our spiritual DNA kits revealing that we are of the same lineage. We share the same DNA as we are members of the family of Christ. What a great blessing to have relatives throughout the world that we can call family.

### Scripture Reference: Mark 3:35

"Whoever does God's will is my brother and sister and mother."

### Prayer:

*Heavenly Father, thank you for adopting me into Your family. I know you chose me as your daughter. I love you in Jesus' name. Amen.*

## *Reflections*

# Day 13

**Joshua 1:9**

# DAY 13
# FEAR—YES YOU CAN

*"Didn't I tell you _____?!"* Almost everyone has heard this at least once. Growing up, I can admit that I heard it more than once, and usually it was in the sound of my mother's voice. I was usually being chastised for something that I was told to do that I didn't do. Sometimes I had what I thought was a good reason for not doing whatever it was I was asked to do. In fact, there were times I thought I had a better plan. (Like the time I tried to thaw a chicken to prep it for frying by putting it in boiling water in a plastic bag.) There were even times when I was afraid that I couldn't complete a task. There were still other instances when I didn't think I should have to do something, and there are other times I just didn't feel like doing it.

As I've matured, I realize my mother knew what she wanted me to do and - often before I realized - that I was capable of performing the task. Here's the thing, whether it's fear, disobedience, pride, or any other issue that's causing you not to do anything that is a command from someone in authority, there is generally a negative consequence for disobeying the command. Instead of enduring that negative consequence, consider this option: Submit to authority and obey the command. God is the ultimate authority, and He will only instruct or command you to do what He knows you have the capacity to do. In addition, He will be there with you the entire way.

### Scripture Reference: Joshua 1:9

"Have I not commanded you? Be strong and courageous. Do not be afraid; do not be discouraged, for the Lord your God will be with you wherever you go."

### Prayer:

*Father, thank you for reminding me that I am strong and courageous. I know I can do this! In Jesus' name. Amen.*

## *Reflections*

# Day 14

**Isaiah 41:10**

# DAY 14
# FEAR—THE TEST

Have you ever met anyone that has test anxiety? As a corporate trainer, I administer an exam after each class. I tell the audience that we will have an assessment at the end of the course that covers some of the material we've learned that day. In addition, I inform them that we will do a review prior to the assessment and that the assessment is open book, open notes, and open system. I also let them know that, to a certain degree, it is open instructor. This means that they can ask for clarity about a question that I will explain if they are uncertain what the question is asking.

With all of the above, it seems that taking the assessment would be a breeze. Well, I've met some students that freeze up and seem to forget everything they've been taught. Some won't go forward, will not read their notes or book, nor will they even look in the system that is in front of them. Some try to get through as quickly as possible and answer questions quickly without reading them. Generally, the result is the same - failure. What's amazing is that at their request, I will sit beside the same people, and jokingly say that I will stare at their computer for them. When I do this, they usually answer correctly.

Often those that failed initially, score 100% on a subsequent try! Apparently, some people feel more comfortable knowing I am next to them as they go through the assessment. Most tests do not require a 100% score to pass and are designed to assess what you learned from a particular teaching, not whether you're an expert. Expert status comes from experience. Consider this, every failure is not because you don't know the answer. Some are because you're afraid of the test.

### Scripture Reference: Isaiah 41:10

"So do not fear, for I am with you; do not be dismayed, for I am your God.

I will strengthen you and help you; I will uphold you with my righteous right hand."

### Prayer:

*Father, thank you for teaching me, training me, and holding my hand during every test. I know by faith you are with me. In Jesus' name. Amen.*

## *Reflections*

# Day 15

Philippians 4:13

# DAY 15
# FEAR—SENDING A SHOUT OUT TO FEAR

It was 2:30 p.m. and the flight was scheduled to depart fifteen minutes later. At the speed that I was moving, I was likely going to miss my flight! The flight was the last one to Houston, and if I missed it, I would need to try to get another flight the next day. That would cost me another night's hotel fee, less time at home, and a bunch of problems in general. My son says that I get to the airport way too early. Well, that's by design. I don't like to be rushed with anything as I'm usually very laidback and do most things at a leisurely pace. However, everything was outside of my control that day since traffic was a beast, and I arrived at the airport late.

The thoughts running through my head that day about missing my flight lit a fire under me, and leisure was not an option. If I had any chance of making the flight, I had to move at least twice as fast as I usually did. I started to semi-jog/trot/run and moved myself, my backpack, and my carryon bag at a pace that I didn't even know I was capable of executing.

I made it to the gate just in time and was able to make it home without any more drama. The fear of missing my flight set me into motion and propelled me in a way that was awesome. I experienced strength that I know only God could grant.

**Scripture Reference: Philippians 4:13**

"I can do all things through him who gives me strength."

**Prayer:**

*Father, thank you for bringing my strength to the surface and renewing my confidence. In Jesus' name. Amen.*

## *Reflections*

# Day 16

**Ephesians 3:20**

# DAY 16
# FEAR—MORE THAN I ASKED FOR

Have you ever been afraid, anxious, or worried? I have. Truthfully, I was so fearful in one area that it actually caused me to have difficulty sleeping one night! For anyone that knows me, this was major because one area that I do not have difficulty is sleeping. As a matter of fact, I don't necessarily have to be sleepy to go to sleep. I can tell myself to go to sleep, and I basically sleep on demand. Well, this day I couldn't sleep because I was fearful and began to worry. A scene that caused me to be afraid was playing on repeat in my head, and I couldn't get it to stop. I knew I needed help. Therefore, I asked God for peace.

What He gave me was the word *shalom.* Shalom means peace. It also means much more than that! **According to Strong's Concordance 7965,** s*halom* means "completeness, wholeness, health, peace, welfare, safety soundness, tranquility, prosperity, perfectness, fullness, rest, harmony, the absence of agitation or discord." How grateful I am that God heard my prayer, granted my request, and added more than I asked for! He's willing to do the same for you.

## Scripture Reference: Ephesians 3:20

"Now to him who is able to do immeasurably more than all we ask or imagine, according to his power that is at work within us."

## Prayer:

*Father, thank you for this perfect gift of Shalom. I receive it in Jesus' name. Amen.*

## *Reflections*

# Day 17

**Proverbs 18:12**

# DAY 17
# FEAR—JUST DO IT

How many times have you decided not to pursue something because you were afraid of the outcome? There is always a sense of uncertainty when we take on a new task, whether that's starting a new career, traveling to a distant land, pursuing a new hobby, changing a hairstyle, purchasing a new home, or even starting a family. Often, the preventive to fulfilling desires that we hope for is because there is a sense of fear of the unknown. Fear can show up in many ways including never starting and/or finishing something that you've spent many days and nights thinking and dreaming about. One thing is certain, if you never start, you'll never finish. Are you the next bestselling author, entrepreneur, furniture maker, homeowner, wife, husband, parent or whatever else you've been hoping for? Take time today to consider a dream that you've hoped for, and make the necessary steps to move forward. Don't think or rationalize yourself out of it. Don't continue to dream about it as if it's impossible. Just do it.

**Scripture Reference: Proverbs 13:12**

"Hope deferred makes the heart sick, but a longing fulfilled is a tree of life."

**Prayer:**

*Father, I realize that time runs out quickly. I want to see the dreams and goals that you've placed in my heart come to pass. I trust you to use me. In Jesus' name. Amen.*

## *Reflections*

# Day 18

**Matthew 25:15-18**

# DAY 18
# FEAR—DIG IT UP

Have you ever hidden something of value for safe keeping and realized that you hid it so deep that you hid it from yourself? If you've ever done that, it can be frustrating when you realize that you need what you've hidden, yet you can't find it. You were given talents that have value and should be used and increase. The same holds true when we hide our talents instead of using them as God intended for us to do so. Go out today with your shovel and dig up the buried talents you hid for safekeeping. It is now time to take those hidden talents and increase them so the Master will be pleased with your work.

### Scripture Reference: Matthew 25:15-18

"<sup>15</sup> And unto one he gave five talents, to another two, and to another one; to every man according to his several ability; and straightway took his journey. <sup>16</sup> Then he that had received the five talents went and traded with the same, and made them other five talents. <sup>17</sup> And likewise he that had received two, he also gained other two. <sup>18</sup> But he that had received one went and digged in the earth, and hid his lord's money."

**Prayer:**

*Father, I'm sorry. I didn't trust myself to be able to do some of the things you've told me I could do. I didn't always know that You would work through me, and that I was not to depend on my capability alone. I'm putting my trust in you and your abilities and telling pride to go so you will be pleased with me! In Jesus' name. Amen.*

## Reflections

# Day 19

2 Corinthians 9:9-11

# DAY 19

# FINANCES—GENEROSITY

Generosity has its rewards. Some say it this way - you can't beat God giving. In your scripture reference today, we can see that the poor are benefited as their need is met. The generous sower is also replenished with more seed for the generous giver to sow, more bread representing God meeting the needs of life for the sower, as well as enlarging their harvest of righteousness.

The Scripture indicates that those that are generous will be able to give generously on every occasion. Because of their generosity towards others, God receives thanksgiving. This displays an awesome cycle of giving to others, their needs being met, our needs being met and exceeded, and God being thanked because He used your generosity to meet the needs of others.

### Scripture Reference: 2 Corinthians 9:9-11

"[9] As it is written: "They have freely scattered their gifts to the poor; their righteousness endures forever. [10] Now he who supplies seed to the sower and bread for food will also supply and increase your store of seed and will enlarge the harvest of your righteousness. [11] You will be enriched in every way so that you can be generous on every occasion, and through us your generosity will result in thanksgiving to God."

**Prayer:**

*Father, thank you for trusting me to sow and reap. Your generosity is manifested to others through me. Continue to pour into me, and I will pour out to others so that you will get the glory through the thanksgiving that is offered up to you. In Jesus' name. Amen.*

## *Reflections*

# Day 20

Exodus 34:4; Matthew 19:21-26;
Psalm 112:1-3; Deuteronomy 8:17-18

# DAY 20
# FINANCES—GOD 1ST

God is not opposed to wealth. It is possible to be rich and please God. Wealth in itself is not the issue. God's position in relationship to man's wealth however can be. Wealth cannot become more important than God. (Exodus 34:14; Matthew 19:21-26) If God were opposed to wealth, He wouldn't call those that fear Him blessed, nor would He decree wealth and riches in their house (Psalm 112:1-3) Furthermore, He wouldn't declare that He gave us the ability to create or produce wealth and show it as a covenant made with our ancestors (Deuteronomy 8:17-18)

**Scripture References:**

**Exodus 34:14** "Do not worship any other god, for the Lord, whose name is Jealous, is a jealous God."

**Matthew 19:21-26** "[21] Jesus answered, 'If you want to be perfect, go, sell your possessions and give to the poor, and you will have treasure in heaven. Then come, follow me.' [22] When the young man heard this, he went away sad, because he had great wealth. [23] Then Jesus said to his disciples, 'Truly I tell you, it is hard for someone who is rich to enter the kingdom of heaven. [24] Again I tell you, it is easier for a camel to go through the eye of a needle than for someone who is rich to enter the kingdom of God.' ²⁵ When the disciples heard this, they were greatly astonished and asked, 'Who then can be saved?' ²⁶ Jesus looked at them and said, 'With man this is impossible, but with God all things are possible.' "

**Psalm 112:1-3** "¹ Praise the Lord. Blessed are those who fear the Lord, who find great delight in his commands. ² Their children will be mighty in the land; the generation of the upright will be blessed. ³ Wealth and riches are in their houses, and their righteousness endures forever."

**Deuteronomy 8:17-18** "¹⁷ You may say to yourself, "My power and the strength of my hands have produced this wealth for me." ¹⁸ But remember the Lord your God, for it is he who gives you the ability to produce wealth, and so confirms his covenant, which he swore to your ancestors, as it is today."

**Prayer:**

*Heavenly Father, thank you for showing me that wealth in itself is not bad. Thank you for letting me know that your desire is to take care of us in every manner including financially. Thank you for delivering me from a mind of poverty and keeping me with the understanding that in everything you are number one. In Jesus' name. Amen.*

## *Reflections*

# Day 21

**Proverbs 10:22**

# DAY 21
# FINANCES—MIKEY RICH

Many of you may have heard of the character Richie Rich. There was a movie, a cartoon show and even comic books featuring the character. Richie Rich was the wealthiest kid in the world and had access to everything a kid could ever want because his father was a billionaire businessman and philanthropist. My son's name is Michael, or Mike as we call him. He's an adult now, but when he was very young, under age 10 or so, he told his dad and me about some things he wanted us to get for him. We didn't generally lavish him with exceptionally expensive gifts, but this day he shared his wants with us. I can't tell you today exactly what all those things were, but I remember him mentioning a Lamborghini car being on the list as a gift for graduation. My husband and I couldn't hold it back. We laughed out loud at his request. Mike didn't seem to be phased, although he looked like he didn't know what the inside joke was. I said, "You must think we're rich." His response was simple, "No, but I know we're wealthy."

I have never forgotten that day because it was a reality check for me. Our son saw us as being able to physically and financially provide whatever he wanted. Furthermore, he made a public declaration that day that I declare and affirm myself today: "We are wealthy!" I'm not saying parents should give their children everything they want, because there are levels of maturity that dictates what each individual can handle. On the other hand, I am saying that our Heavenly Father is capable of providing everything we need and even beyond that to include our desires. There is a need for those of us that are God's children to see him as the loving Father, King, and Great Provider He is. Moreover, we should acknowledge Him in all we do in every area, including financially.

### Scripture Reference: Proverbs 10:22

"The blessing of the Lord brings wealth, without painful toil for it."

### Prayer:

*Heavenly Father, I am your daughter, and I receive all of the benefits of being your child, including your wealth. I count it as a blessing. In Jesus' name. Amen.*

## Reflections

# Day 22

**Malachi 3:10**

# DAY 22
# FINANCES—OLD MATH

The tithe (or ten percent) as a minimum of your income should be considered a responsibility and a privilege. Tithing is given in the Old Testament, but the result of tithing still manifests in our lives today. Many may even argue that since it is Old Testament, it is legalistic and has been fulfilled with the shed blood of Jesus. Well, I tell you this - tithing works! I could personally testify of how the tithe has sustained the other 90% of my family's income when we were barely able to survive and increased it so dramatically that I cannot understand what mathematical formula could be applied! I've even witnessed people that were not members of any local church stop by solely to bring their tithe because it had verified itself as a proven method in their lives. Even our son, as a small child, saw the benefits of tithing (or 'teething' as he called it). After giving 10% of his very small income earned from chores, his tithe unexpectedly and miraculously came back at five times the amount of his full original income within a few days. If you still aren't convinced of the benefits of tithing, the scripture in Malachi allows you to test it out yourself. Go ahead, give it a try. I'm sure you're going to enjoy the blessings that pour out in an overflowing fashion.

## Scripture Reference: Malachi 3:10

"Bring the whole tithe into the storehouse, that there may be food in my house. 'Test me in this,' says the Lord Almighty, 'and see if I will not throw open the floodgates of heaven and pour out so much blessing that there will not be room enough to store it.' "

## Prayer:

*Father, ten percent of what you've given me is a small amount to give back. I don't always understand your ways, but I know they work. Overflow! In Jesus' name. Amen.*

## *Reflections*

# Day 23

**Proverbs 13:11**

# DAY 23
# FINANCES—
# PINCHING PENNIES

*"Coins tossed in a jar on a dresser add up over time. Pennies spend, too."*

*~ Debra D Jones*

A one-year penny savings challenge was made popular on social media. It starts out by adding a penny to the savings on day one and increasing by another penny each day for an entire year. For example, on day two, you would add two pennies, day three you would add three pennies, and so on. On the last day of the year, you add $3.65. Many people can find a penny or two lying around their house or even on the ground, but they may think very little of them because the value of a penny alone is small. However, adding to it daily is the key. Then, it grows and becomes substantial. Some of you have already done the math on the penny challenge. On the last day of the challenge, your total savings is $667.95! I don't know about you, but I believe that is an excellent example of how anyone who doesn't believe they have money to save can start out small and create a substantial savings that didn't hurt in the process. Think of the possibility of using this method to teach young children the power of saving over time.

### Scripture Reference: Proverbs 13:11

"Dishonest money dwindles away, but whoever gathers money little by little makes it grow."

### Prayer:

*Father, I'm not looking for a get rich quick scheme. Thank you for showing me that slow and steady can win the race with notable increase. In Jesus' name. Amen.*

## *Reflections*

# Day 24

**Proverbs 10:4**

# DAY 24
# FINANCES—WORK

**Question:** Why do rich people continue to work when they have more than enough income to sustain them for their entire lives?

**Answer:** Because they are not lazy.

Laziness and diligence are both generally easy to discern. Laziness indicates that someone is unwilling to exert any energy. They don't want to do any work. I've seen them on the job. They actually seem to 'work' harder at being lazy than anything else. Scripture says if a man won't work, don't let him eat. (2 Thessalonians 3:10) Diligence shows care, concern and hardworking characteristics in a man.

The rich man who is not diligent would not be able to maintain his riches if he became lazy. I've seen the diligent worker as well, and many have gone on to amass great incomes. It was not necessarily because their end game was to make more money, but it was because they worked hard, and money was a byproduct of their hard work and character to produce work that they could be proud of in the end. If you're lazy without any desire to do better, know that poverty awaits you. I pray that your desire transforms so that you too may experience all God has available for those that are diligent.

### Scripture Reference: Proverbs 10:4

"Lazy hands make for poverty, but diligent hands bring wealth."

### Prayer:

*Father, I am not lazy. I work diligently to represent you and myself in all I do. Thank you for the wealth that diligence brings. In Jesus' name. Amen.*

## *Reflections*

# Day 25

**James 1:5**

# DAY 25
# LIFE—EARN, LEARN, OR FREE

Today's topic is related to wisdom. Wisdom is generally knowledge, good judgment, sound actions, or experience. We all need wisdom, and we have several ways we can become wise. We can earn it. We can learn it. We can get it for free.

To earn wisdom includes experiences, and sometimes those experiences can be ones when our judgment was not wise. We may make mistakes that can help us in our future decision-making if we take heed. An example would be to turn down an unmarked road and realize that it is a dead end. This requires you to turn around. In the future, when you get to that road, you know not to go that way. To learn wisdom is to be taught based on someone else's experiences and information that is shared. An example would be that someone says, "Don't go down that road. It's unmarked, I've been there before, and that is a dead end. You'll have to turn around." When you use that information to make a sound decision, that displays wisdom.

Free wisdom is a gift from God. It allows you to discern that the juncture that you're at doesn't look or feel like it would be a good option, and you decide not to turn down the road. This wisdom does not rely on experiences or information provided by another human. God gets the glory for providing it, and it is available free of charge. I can say that I've acquired some wisdom in each of these ways. The best wisdom I've used, however, has been the one that didn't cost me but was provided free for the asking. God is willing and able to provide that wisdom for each of us. For that reason, if you need wisdom, ask God who is generous in His giving.

### Scripture Reference: James 1:5

"If any of you lacks wisdom, you should ask God, who gives generously to all without finding fault, and it will be given to you."

### Prayer:

*Father, I ask that you give me wisdom in a generous fashion so I can apply it to any areas needed. In Jesus' name. Amen.*

## *Reflections*

# Day 26

**James 1:9**

## DAY 26
## LIFE— OPEN MOUTH, INSERT FOOT

*"Wise men are not always silent, but they know when to be."*
*~ Unknown*

"Open mouth, insert foot" - This idiom suggests when you open your mouth and say something without sufficient information, what you say can be insulting, hurtful, or plain stupid. I witnessed this one day as I was riding a group shuttle to work. A woman saw a guy through the shuttle window and said something insulting about him. I spoke up and said, "That person appears to be mentally ill. I recognize that behavior. My brother is mentally ill." I wasn't personally insulted, although I believed the woman was insensitive. After I spoke up, the woman sitting next to me was clearly insulted and said, "My father is schizophrenic. He's subject to walk down the street with aluminum foil on his head."

We continued to ride the group shuttle to work for more than a year. If the woman who made the insensitive remark had kept quiet, she would've likely heard snippets of conversation between myself and the other woman about mental illness, and hopefully not allowed that remark to escape her lips. She also may have missed out on a potentially beneficial business connection. Listening is an often underrated and under-developed skill. We would do well to beef up our listening skills, and when we do need to speak, hopefully we would do so with helpful intentions and purpose.

**Scripture Reference: James 1:19**

"My dear brothers and sisters, take note of this: Everyone should be quick to listen, slow to speak and slow to become angry."

**Prayer:**

*Father, it is not my desire to hurt anyone with things I say. I will use my two ears to listen twice as much as I speak. I will also be slow to become angry. In Jesus' name. Amen.*

## *Reflections*

# Day 27

**Philippians 4:13**

# DAY 27
# LIFE—ICAN

*"Whether you think you can, or you think you can't— you're right."*

*~ Henry Ford*

What are you challenged with that seems too difficult? Do you have a task, assignment, goal, or calling that seems overwhelming or impossible when you think about it? The solution to your problem may very well begin in your thought process. As you begin to conceive an idea, especially in an area that may be unchartered territory for you, it may seem too difficult, too uncertain, too much responsibility, too unlikely, too strenuous, too improbable, or even impossible. Too much! Instead of being a victim to negative thinking, capture your thoughts and align them with what God says in Luke 18:27, "What is impossible with man is possible with God." Then, let us pray that for those tasks and assignments that are specifically assigned to us that God gives us the strength to fulfill them, and let us make this declaration: I Can!

### Scripture Reference: Philippians 4:13

"I can do all this through him who gives me strength."

### Prayer:

*Heavenly Father, thank you for my thoughts being conducive to receiving that you're giving me strength to accomplish even difficult tasks. In Jesus' name. Amen.*

## Reflections

# Day 28

**Matthew 6:10; Psalm 34:1**

# DAY 28
# LIFE—I WILL

Before I walked with God, there was a friend that whenever she wanted me to do something for her, she would start off with, *Don't you want to…* My answer to her question was often, "No," because it was based on my desire. If she asked the same question in a different manner *Will you…*, my answer would often be, "Yes." It was based on a conscious decision I made. She realized this over time, and posed her questions in a way that got the results she wanted. You might wonder why a subtle change in the way the question was worded affected my answer. It's because, my want, which was my desire, and my will, which was a decision, did not always agree. As Christians, our wants and will may not always agree. Although the struggle is real, we know that God's will is always best for us. Let us pray that our desire and decisions become more closely aligned.

**Scripture References:**

**Matthew 6:10** "Your kingdom come, your will be done, on earth as it is in heaven."

**Psalm 34:1** "I will extol the Lord at all times; his praise will always be on my lips."

**Prayer:**

*Father, I want my desire to align itself with your desires. When it is difficult for me to even get my will to cooperate, I proclaim not my will but your will be done. In Jesus's name. Amen.*

## *Reflections*

# Day 29

John 9:4

# DAY 29
# LIFE—IMUST

There comes a time in almost everyone's life when they know that there are certain things that really need to happen. When we get to that point, we may feel a deep sense of duty or compulsion to do it. We have, at this point, believed that we can do it. Moreover, we've made a decision that we will do it, but it no longer has a future tense attached to it. We must do it as surely as we must breathe to continue living. The must could be returning to school to pursue a course of study, writing a book, starting a new business, a new career, a new ministry, exercising, or losing weight. The must could be a great many different things. Whatever your must is, it brings you to the point where you realize that you cannot be at rest until you accomplish this particular mission or assignment. Often, we realize these missions or assignments are directing us towards the destiny that God has designed for each of us. Let us ask God to help us stay on course with destiny by doing what we must do.

**Scripture Reference: John 9:4**

"As long as it is day, we must do the works of him who sent me. Night is coming, when no one can work."

**Prayer:**

*Father, I must do what I'm designed to do. I can feel it as surely as I can feel my own hands. Thank you for the push. In Jesus' name. Amen.*

## *Reflections*

# Day 30

**Psalm 121: 1-4**

# DAY 30
# LIFE—
# THE HELP

There was a movie with a title of *The Help* based on a New York Times bestselling novel by the same name. The movie set in Jackson, Mississippi in early 1960s was about African American women who worked as maids for their white employers. During the time the movie was set, the maids were generally spoken of by their employers in a generic sense as "the help." There was some outrage when the movie was released. Some felt the depiction was demeaning and belittling and showed these women as being weak. There was a suggestion that being someone's help was low-class.

I've helped and been helped in many areas of my life. When I've been helped, it has been because I was weak in an area, and I needed assistance. When I've been the helper or assistant, it's been because I was strong in an area that another needed my assistance. God is willing to be our assistant because we are weak. He who has made the heaven and earth, is the Ruler of all. He does not get tired, and He is willing to assist us in every area of our lives. God himself is the Divine Help. Look to Him for all your needs.

### How to Pray When You Don't Have Time

**Scripture Reference: Psalm 121:1-4**

¹"I lift up my eyes to the mountains - where does my help come from? ²My help comes from the Lord, the Maker of heaven and earth. ³He will not let your foot slip - he who watches over you will not slumber; ⁴indeed, he who watches over Israel will neither slumber nor sleep."

**Prayer:**

*Heavenly Father, thank you for showing me that the weak are truly strong. Thank you for allowing me to see that in whatever way I serve others, I can serve you. Thank you for being the Help I need. In Jesus' name. Amen.*

## *Reflections*

# Day 31

# DAY 31
# THE PRAYER

*Heavenly Father,*

*This is the day that you have made. I rejoice and I'm glad in it. As I approach you today, I repent of any sin in my life and ask that by the power Holy Spirit, I am able to walk upright before you. I thank you, Father, that you've been present each day as I've moved through this devotional. The purpose of the devotional was to set aside time for you and me. A few minutes each day has increased my desire to spend even more time with you throughout the day. I find myself thinking of you and wanting to steal away with you. I love you Lord.*

*Thank you for addressing needs in my life in the areas of Faith, Family, Fear, Finances and Life where you knew I needed assistance. Your solutions are much easier than I ever thought they would be. As I continue to spend time with you, I am encouraged by my eyes being opened to the areas where I excel as well as in those that I need to grow. I have time for you, Lord. I have time to adore and worship you, as well as time to receive your love, wisdom, instruction and correction for my life. Bless anyone that thinks they don't have time to pray by giving them the desire to pray. I love you forever. In Jesus' name. Amen.*

## *Reflections*

## *Reflections*

# ABOUT THE AUTHOR

Debra D. Jones is a wife, mother, corporate trainer and Minister of the Gospel of Jesus Christ. She is the youngest of 8 children born and raised in Chicago, Illinois. She is the host of Periscope's *"Can You Pray 5 Minutes?"* and serves at her home Church, First Metropolitan Church in Houston, Texas.

She has taken the vision of creating a devotional to address the everyday needs of busy people and encourage them to develop a consistent prayer life by publishing *How to Pray When You Don't Have Time: A Devotional.*

She enjoys events with family and friends and spending time with her husband Bill and son Michael.

www.ingramcontent.com/pod-product-compliance
Lightning Source LLC
Chambersburg PA
CBHW070919160426
43193CB00011B/1528